Chatterbox

PUPIL'S BOOK 1   Derek Strange

Oxford University Press

Oxford University Press
Walton Street, Oxford OX2 6DP

Oxford   New York   Toronto
Delhi Bombay Calcutta Madras Karachi
Petaling Jaya Singapore Hong Kong Tokyo
Nairobi Dar es Salaam Cape Town
Melbourne Auckland

and associated companies in
Berlin Ibadan

OXFORD and OXFORD ENGLISH are trade
marks of Oxford University Press

ISBN 0 19 432431 1

© Derek Strange 1989

First published 1989
Fourth impression 1990

The main illustrations in this book are by Bucket.

The story page illustrations are by Christyan Jones.

The illustration on page 32 is by Kay Smith.

Photography is by Mark Mason and Libby Howells.
The publishers would like to thank Rex Features
for permission to reproduce a photograph.

'Happy Birthday to you' (© 1935 Sammy Birchard Co. USA)
is reproduced by permission of Keith Prowse Music Pub.
Co. Ltd, London.

Printed in Hong Kong

What's your name?

 1 Listen and repeat.

I'm = I am

♫ **a...b...c...d...**

2 Listen and sing.

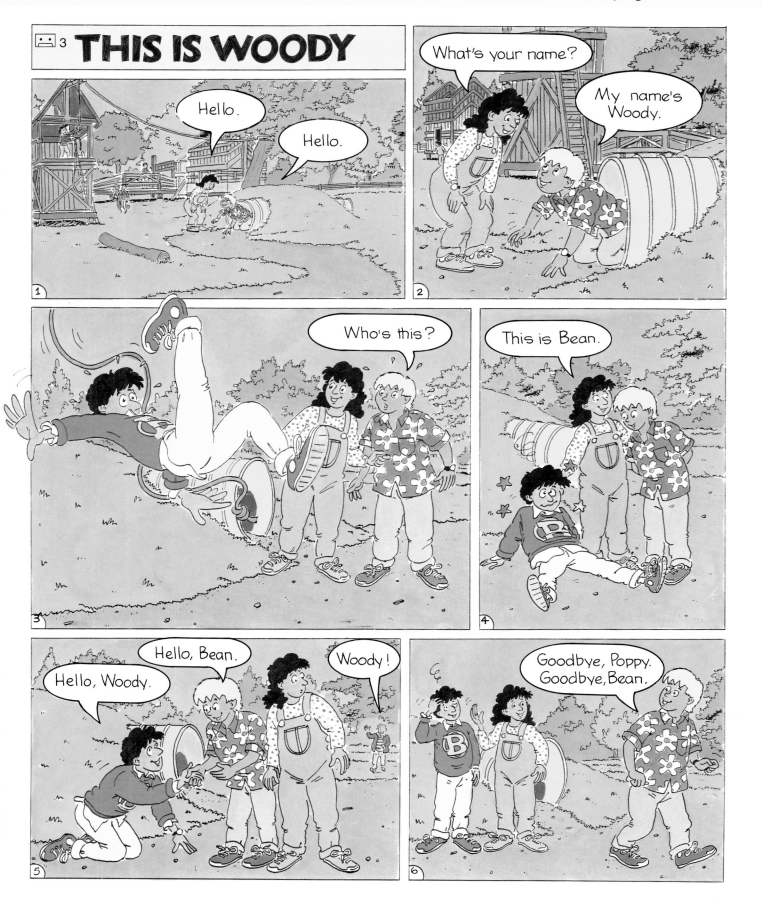

Who's this?

Read and match.

Zoko   Woody   Bean   Poppy

Listen, please

📼 4 Listen, look and point.

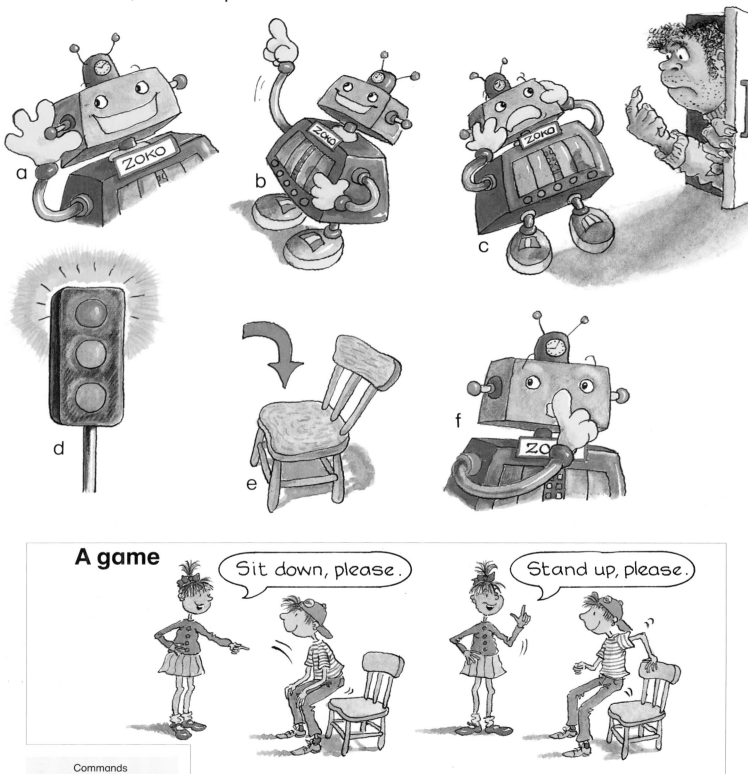

A game

Sit down, please.

Stand up, please.

Commands

What's this?

Look and say.

 a pencil

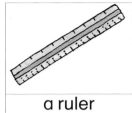 a ruler

 a bag

 a pen

 a book

 a rubber

 a cassette

 a desk

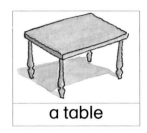 a table

Now ask and answer.

What's this?

A pen.

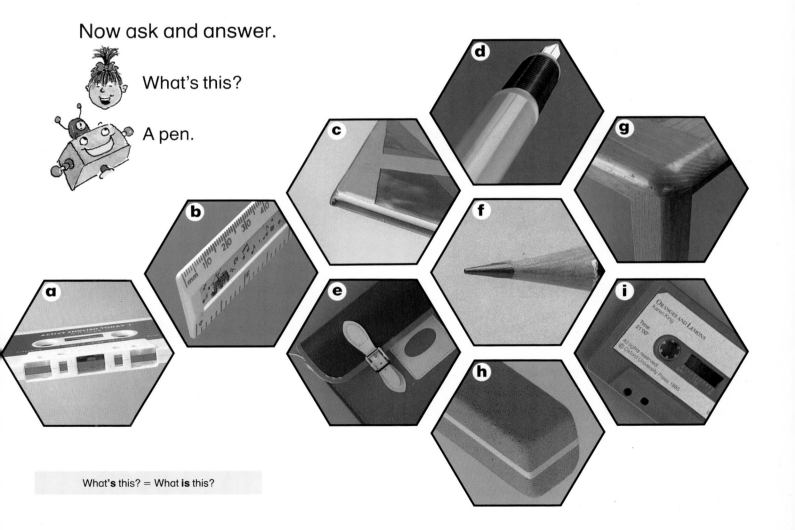

What's this? = What is this?

♫ How are you?

📼 6 Listen and sing.

Good morning, good morning.
How are you? How are you?
I'm fine, thank you.

Good afternoon, good afternoon.
How are you? How are you?
I'm fine, thank you.

Good morning, good morning.
How are you? How are you?
I'm fine. Goodbye.
Goodbye . . . goodbye . . . goodbye . . .

Language puzzle

Read and match.

a. Good . . .   . . . are you?
b. How . . .   . . . thanks.
c. Fine, thank . . . . . . morning.
d. I'm fine, ... you.
e. Here! . . .   . . . Thank you.

Numbers

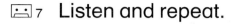 7 Listen and repeat.

one's a number,

two's a number,

three's a number,

four!

number **five** is under **six**,

and number **seven**'s more!

eight's a number,

nine's a number,

now we come to **ten** . . .

and we're back at **one** again!

Numbers 1 – 10

HOW OLD ARE YOU?

An apple, an icecream

Look and say.

an apple   **an e**lephant   **an i**cecream   **an o**range   **an u**mbrella

A game: Find . . . an elephant

Point and say.

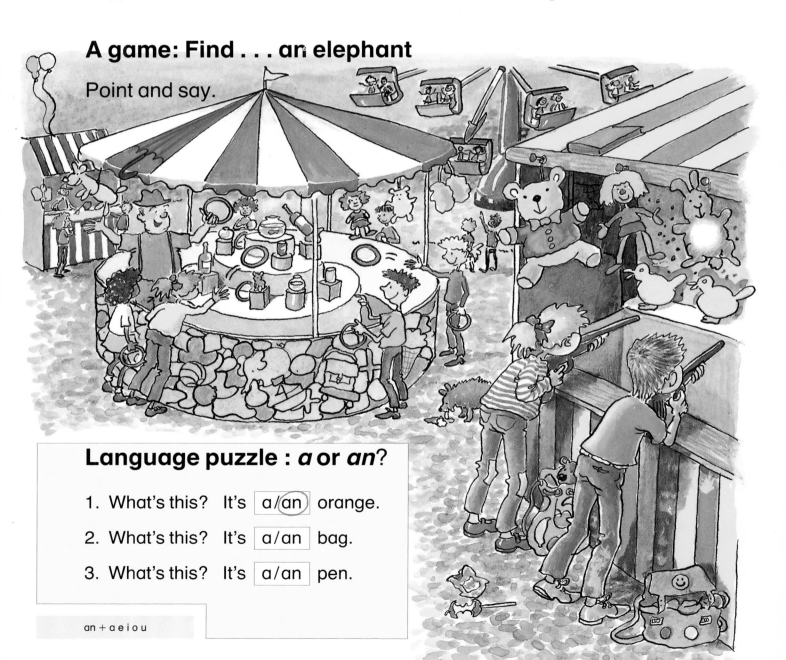

Language puzzle : *a* or *an*?

1. What's this? It's [a / an] orange.

2. What's this? It's [a / an] bag.

3. What's this? It's [a / an] pen.

an + a e i o u

Phone numbers

Look and say.

26430	85791	63692
39642	51078	99284

Hello? This is 94312

9 Listen and match.

1.

Hello? This is ...

75868

2.

Hello? This is ...

90632

3.

Hello? This is ...

94312

4.

Hello? This is ...

75408

Unit 4

Happy birthday!

⊡ 10 Listen, look and point.   Then ask and answer.

What's this?

It's a kite.

a balloon

a doll

a kite

a bicycle

a boat

a car

a ball

a football

an aeroplane

a computer

It's a . . . = It is a . . .

11 IT'S A BALLOON

A game: What's this?

♪ **Happy birthday to you!**

😐 12 Listen and sing.

Happy birthday
  to you!
Happy birthday
  to you!
Happy birthday
  to Poppy!
Happy birthday
  to Bean!

It's a/an . . .

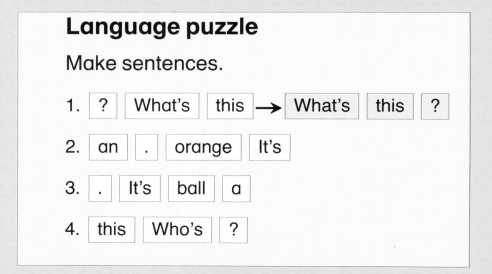

Language puzzle

Make sentences.

1. | ? | What's | this | → | What's | this | ? |

2. | an | . | orange | It's |

3. | . | It's | ball | a |

4. | this | Who's | ? |

A game: Listen and find

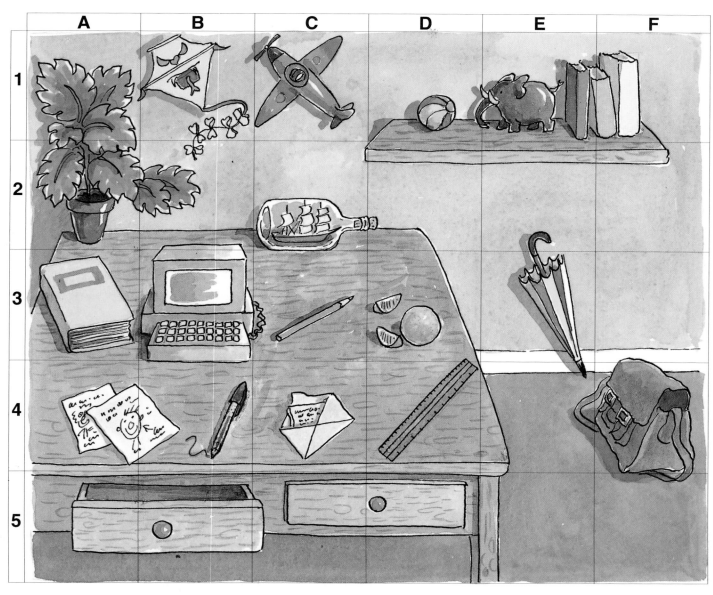

This is Kate . . . She's eight

⊡ 13 Listen and point.   Then listen and answer.

1 Hello, I'm Kate. I'm eight.

This is Kate. She's eight.

2 Good morning, I'm Ken. I'm ten.

This is Ken. He's ten.

3 Hi, I'm Caroline. I'm nine.

This is Caroline. She's nine.

4 I'm Kevin. I'm seven. I'm a hippopotamus.

This is Kevin. He's seven. He's a hippopotamus.

He's . . ./She's . . . = He is . . ./She is . . .

THE RIVER CAFÉ

His bicycle . . . Her bicycle

Look and say.

This is Ken.

This is Kate.

This is **his** bicycle.

This is **her** bicycle.

Now read and match.

1. This is his ruler.   d
2. This is his balloon.
3. This is his cassette.
4. This is his bag.
5. This is his envelope.

6. This is her ruler.
7. This is her balloon.
8. This is her cassette.
9. This is her bag.
10. This is her envelope.

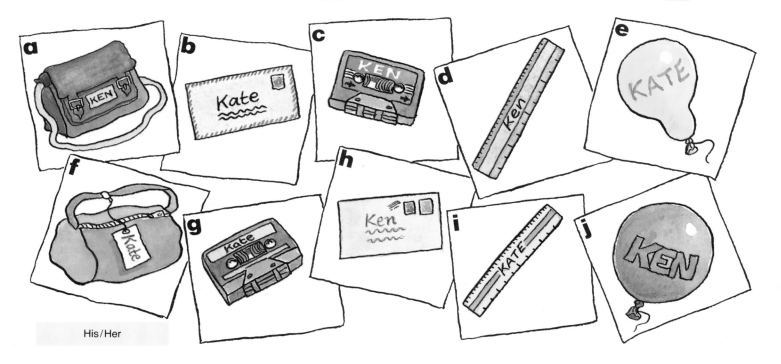

His / Her

Bingo! *(Revision)*

a ruler	an aeroplane	a ball	an envelope
an icecream	a book	a car	a pencil
a computer	a kite	a cassette	an apple
a boat	an umbrella	a doll	a bag
a desk	an orange	a rubber *eraser*	an elephant
a table	a balloon	a bicycle	a pen

Is it an aeroplane?

Ask and answer.

 Is it an aeroplane? *airplane*

 No, it isn't.

 Is it a hippo?

Yes, it is.

15 Now listen and point to the right picture.

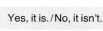
Is it . . . ?   Yes, it is. / No, it isn't.

THE DETECTIVE

The small box and the big box

 17 Listen, look and point.

a

Here's the big box.

b

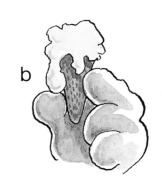

c

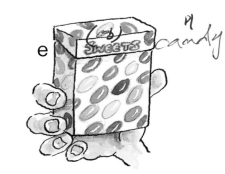

d

e

f

g

h

Now ask and answer.

 What's this?

 It's the big box.

the . . .   Adjective + noun

Language puzzle

Read and match.

1. It's . . .   . . . it isn't.
2. Is this . . .   . . . the big television.
3. No, ... it is.
4. Yes, ... the small icecream?

♫ The happy hippo

📻 18 Listen and sing.

Hippo – pota – pota – mus
I'm the hippo – pota – mus
Hippo – pota – happiness
I'm the happy hippo!

Happy ele – elephant
You and me and me and you,
Come and sing this happy song
With the happy hippo!

You say it!

Hello. Here's Henry the happy hippopotamus!

Unit 7

I've got a big nose

Look and say.

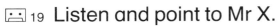 19 **Listen and point to Mr X.**

I've got . . . = I have got . . .

MR X IS IN LONDON

This is my family

Read.

This is my family.

This is my mother, Ellen. She's got big eyes.

This is my father, Ernie. He's got big ears.

This is my sister, Annie. She's got a small mouth.

This is my friend, Nick. He's got a small nose.

I've got two brothers. Herman is nine and Shep is ten. Herman has got long hair and Shep has got short hair.

She**'s** got . . . = She **has** got . . .   He**'s** got . . . = He **has** got . . .

A game: Who am I?

Annie

Shep

Herman

Lucy

21 **Listen. Then play the game.**

YOU ARE HERMAN

OK. I'm Herman.

Are you a girl?

No, I'm not a girl.

Are you a boy?

Yes, I am.

Are you nine?

Yes, I am.

You're Herman!

Right! Well done! I'm Herman.

Unit 8

Have you got your bag?

22 Listen and point to the right bag.

> Have you got your book?
>
> Yes, I have.
>
> Have you got a pencil?
>
> No, I haven't.

Now ask and answer.

 Has she got her umbrella?

 Yes, she has.

 Has she got her ruler?

 No, she hasn't.

Have you got . . . ?   Yes, I have. / No, I haven't.

23 THEY'VE GOT CAPTAIN SHADOW

Old and young, fat and thin

Look and say.

| tall | short |

| fat | thin |

| young | old |

| happy | sad |

♫ The family song

📺 24 Listen and sing.

Uncle Paul is young and tall, A–E–I–O–U
Auntie Lynn is old and thin, A–E–I–O–U
    Young and tall, Uncle Paul
    Old and thin, Auntie Lynn
Cousin Pat is short and fat, A–E–I–O–U
And my old Dad is big and sad, A–E–I–O–U
    Short and fat, Cousin Pat
    Big and sad, my old Dad
And Cousin Daisy's lazy!

Adjectives

Two faces

Read.

This is Mutu.
He's got long hair.
He's got big eyes.
He's got a small nose.
He's got a big mouth.

This is Devi.
She's got long hair.
She's got a big nose.
She's got a big mouth.

Now read and answer:

Yes, he has. / No, he hasn't. or: *Yes, she has. / No, she hasn't.*

1 Has Mutu got long hair?
2 Has Devi got short hair?
3 Has Mutu got a happy face?
4 Has Devi got a sad face?
5 Has Devi got big ears?
6 Has Mutu got a big mouth?

 # Unit 9

Can you see an elephant?

Ask and answer.

 Can you see an elephant?

 Yes, I can.

 Can you see a dog?

 No, I can't.

♫ **The zoo song**

⊡ 25 Listen and sing.

Can you see the monkey in her cage?
Can you see the monkey in her cage?
Can you see the monkey . . .
Can you see the monkey . . .
Can you see the monkey in her cage?

Can you hear the lion in his cage?
Can you hear the lion in his cage?
Can you hear the lion . . .
Can you hear the lion . . .
Can you hear the lion in his cage?

Can you . . . ?   Yes, I can./No, I can't.

📻 26 MR X'S PLAN

1. Poppy, Bean! You're here. Well done!

2. Quick! Come on, Captain!

Look! An envelope...

3. Look, Captain! I've got an envelope...

4. ...and a photograph. Who's this?

It's Lifter. She's Mr X's friend.

5. And what's this?

It's a map.

6. Can you read this name?

Yes, I can. Big City Bank.

7. Perhaps this is his plan. Perhaps we can catch Mr X now.

Whose cage is this?

⌣ 27 **Listen and match.**

Monkey's Cage

Bird's Cage

Giraffe's Cage

Snake's Cage

Hippo's Cage

Lion's Cage

This isn't my cage. This is the bird's cage.

Whose . . . ?   It's the _____ 's.

Turn left, turn right

Look and say.

| Turn left | Go straight on | Stop | Turn right |

Can you find the cage?

28 Listen and find the cage.   Then play the game.

Colours

Look and say.

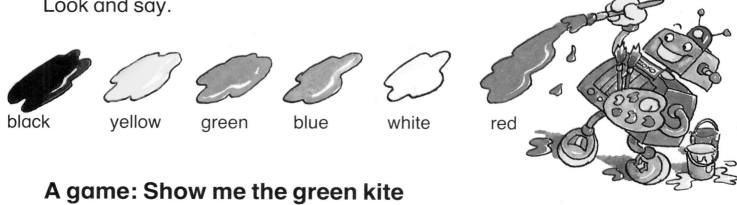

black   yellow   green   blue   white   red

A game: Show me the green kite

□ 29 Listen, look and point.   Then play the game.

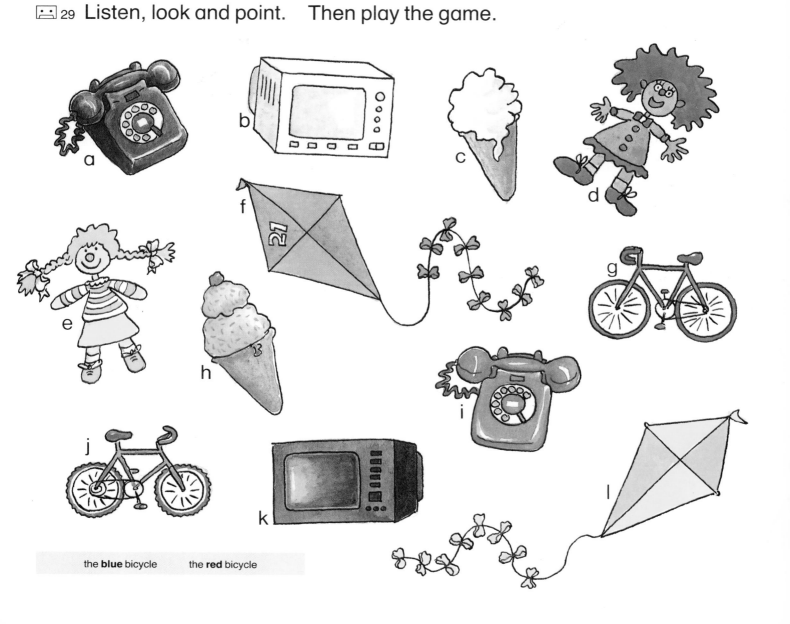

the **blue** bicycle   the **red** bicycle

THE BIG WHITE BOAT

The clothes rhyme

31 Listen and repeat.

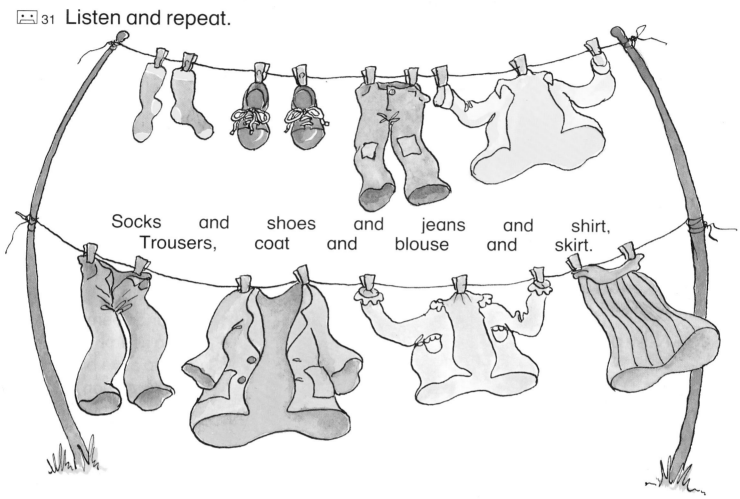

Socks   and   shoes   and   jeans   and   shirt,
Trousers,   coat   and   blouse   and   skirt.

Language puzzle: Who is it?

Read and match.

a black coat
a red skirt
a white blouse
a pair of yellow socks
a pair of red shoes

What colour is . . .?   It's red.

Lucy   Daisy   Shep   Annie

🔲 34 CAN YOU SEE THE BALLOONS?

What colour is Kate's parrot?

🔊 35 Listen and point to Kate's parrot.

Can you find my parrot, please?

He's got brown legs.

Language puzzle

Make sentences.

1. is | ? | colour | your | What | parrot

→ What | colour | is | your | parrot | ?

2. Kate's | ? | Can | parrot | find | you

3. his | What | is | nose | ? | colour

4. shoulders | got | . | He's | red

5. orange | is | . | nose | His

Bob the Bad Banana

Read.

**Find this banana
His name is 'B.B.B.'**

He is a very dangerous banana.
He is from Africa but now he is in England.
He is lazy but he is very clever.
He has got a very big red nose and brown hair.
His coat is yellow and black.
He has got a good friend in England, and his friend is clever and dangerous.
Detectives cannot catch 'B.B.B.' or his friend.
Help us to find 'B.B.B.' and his friend.

Signed: _____.   Date: _____

Now answer the questions.

1. Is B.B.B. from England or from Africa?
2. Has B.B.B. got an orange nose or a red nose?
3. Is B.B.B.'s friend dangerous?
4. Is B.B.B.'s coat yellow and black, or red and brown?
5. Can detectives catch B.B.B. and his friend?

Unit 12

There are five rabbits in the hat

Look and say.

There's one
rabbit in the hat.

There's one
bird in the cage.

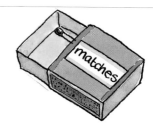

There's one
match in the box.

Now there are five
rabbit**s** in the hat.

Now there are three
bird**s** in the cage.

Now there are ten
match**es** in the box.

A game: Can you remember?

Point and say. *There's a parrot.*

Then close your book and play the game.

There**'s** a . . . = There **is** a . . .   There **are** . . .

LET'S FOLLOW

My uncle's hat

Ask and answer.

　Is there a dog in my hat?

　No, there isn't.

　Is there a rabbit in my hat?

　Yes, there is.

1. Is there a bird on my shoulder?
2. Is there a bag on the table?
3. Is there a book in the bag?
4. Is there a monkey in the bag?
5. Is there a snake in the monkey's socks?

♫ Song

🎞 37 Listen and sing.

There's a pink and yellow rabbit in my uncle's hat,
There's a fat and happy elephant in there too,
There's a brown and orange monkey in my uncle's hat,
And my uncle's hat is blue, blue, blue,
And my uncle's hat is BLUE!

There are nine white lions in my uncle's hat,
There are seven green snakes in there too,
There are six tall giraffes in my uncle's hat,
And my uncle's hat is blue, blue, blue,
And my uncle's hat is BLUE!

Is there . . . ?　　Yes, there is./No, there isn't.

London's parks

Read.

London is a very big city. There are three big parks in London. There is Hyde Park, there is St James's Park, and there is ▽ Regent's Park.

◁ London's famous zoo is in Regent's Park. In the zoo there are animals from Africa, from Asia, from America and from Europe. There are big birds and long snakes in cages. There are hippos and elephants, and you can give bananas to the monkeys!

◁ In the parks you can play football, you can watch the ducks, you can read your book or you can walk.

Answer: right (√) or wrong (×)?

1. There are six big parks in London. . . . . √ ⊗
2. London's famous zoo is in St James's Park. . . . . √ ⊠
3. There are elephants and hippos in the zoo in Regent's Park. . . . √ ×
4. You can play games in the parks in London. . . . . √ ×
5. You can see ducks in the parks in London. . . . . √ ⊠
6. There are parks in my city. . . . . √ ⊠
7. There is a zoo in my city. . . . . √ ×

Unit 13

How many monsters are there?

Ask and answer.

 How many monsters are there in your picture?

 One.

 How many girls are there?

Two.

 38 Now listen and point to the right picture.

How many . . . ?

AT THE SUPERMARKET

Space City

Look at the picture.　Ask and answer.

How many cars can you see?

I can see two.

40 Listen. Answer *Yes* or *No*.

There's a book shop in the street.

Yes, there is.

There are two yellow cars in the street.

No, there aren't.

How many . . . can you see?

Shops: A reading game

Play the game with a friend.

START HERE

You are at the river. GO to the Bird's Cage Café.

The Bird's Cage Café
Meet a friend here.
STOP for an icecream.
Then GO to the Pizza Restaurant.

The Pizza Restaurant
STOP. You are hungry.
Eat a big pizza.
Then GO to the book shop.

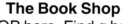

The Clothes Shop
STOP and find a new shirt and a new pair of shoes here.
Then take a bus and GO to the supermarket.

The Book Shop
STOP here. Find a book.
Then take a taxi and GO straight on to the clothes shop.

The Supermarket
STOP. You've got a problem. You haven't got a basket.
Wait here for your sister. She's got a big basket.
Then GO to the bank.

The Bank
STOP here. Is your friend here?
Are you ready?
OK. GO to the cinema now.

The REX Cinema
You're here. Well done!
Now you can see the film with your friend.

FINISH

Unit 14

What time is it?

Look and say.

A	B	C	D	E
	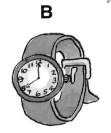			
It's five o'clock.	It's eight o'clock.	It's eleven o'clock.	It's nine o'clock.	It's twelve o'clock.

41 Now listen and point to the right time.

①

②

③

④

It's . . . o'clock.

42 BANANA ICECREAM
Eat the chocolates, Lifter.
But boss...OK, boss.
What time is it, Lifter?
It's ten o'clock, boss.
OK. Now listen. This is the plan...
At eleven o'clock come to the bank with me. Bring the box and the rope.
It's a pretty rope, boss.
Yes. In the bank put the box and the letter on the desk. Here's the letter.
Put the money in the box now.
Now the chocolates, Lifter. Eat the chocolates.
OK, Lifter. Let's go. It's eleven o'clock.
Yes. I've got the rope and the box, boss.
Look! Lifter has got her rope and the box. Have you got the banana icecream, Woody?
Yes. I've got the banana icecream here, Captain.
We're ready for you, Mr X.

when a? the?

♫ The clock song

📼 43 Listen and sing.

It's seven o'clock in the morning,
Get up, get up, get up!
It's seven o'clock, it's eight o'clock,
It's seven, it's eight—Come on! It's late!

It's ten o'clock in the morning,
Tick tock, tick tock, tick tock!
It's ten o'clock, it's nine o'clock,
It's ten, it's nine—Come on! What's the time?

It's nine o'clock in the evening,
Good night, good night, good night!
It's nine o'clock, it's time for bed,
It's nine o'clock—Go on! Go to bed!
Good night, good night, good night!

. . . in the morning   . . . in the evening

Language puzzle

Read and match.

1. It's seven o'clock.
2. It's twelve o'clock.
3. It's eight o'clock.
4. It's eleven o'clock.
5. It's three o'clock.

A game: What's in your box?

Choose four squares together.

Then ask and answer.

 Have you got Lifter's socks in your box?

 No, I haven't.

 Have you got Lifter's letter in your box?

Yes, I have.

Lifter's socks	Mr X's bicycle	Poppy's letter	Woody's photo
Mr X's letter	Poppy's photo	Woody's socks	Lifter's bicycle
Poppy's socks	Woody's bicycle	Lifter's letter	Mr X's photo
Woody's letter	Lifter's photo	Mr X's socks	Poppy's bicycle

Unit 15

Zoko's pictures

📻 44 Listen and point to the right picture.   Then answer the questions.

A

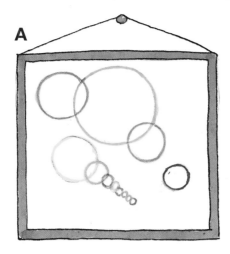

B

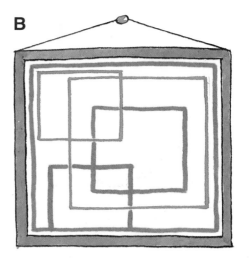

Circles
1. How many circles are there in the picture?
2. How many green circles can you find?

Squares
3. How many squares can you see in the picture?

C

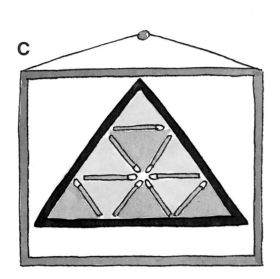

Triangles
4. How many triangles can you find?
5. How many pink triangles are there in the picture?
6. How many grey triangles are there in the picture?

📼 45 NOW, WOODY!

Look again, please *(Revision)*

Be

I am . . .	= I'm . . .
You are . . .	= You're . . .
He is . . .	= He's . . .
She is . . .	= She's . . .
We are . . .	= We're . . .
You are . . .	= You're . . .
They are . . .	= They're . . .

Are you Woody?
> No, I'm not. I'm Bean.

Is she Captain Shadow?
> No, she isn't. She's Lifter.

Check Look again at
pages 1, 3, 10, and 17.

Can

I can see an elephant.
She can see a monkey.
They can see a parrot.

Can you see an elephant?
> Yes, I can. / No, I can't.

Can Mr X read the map?
> Yes, he can. / No, he can't.

Check Look at page 33 again.
Sing the song.

Have got

I have got . . .	= I've got . . .
You have got . . .	= You've got . . .
✓ He has got . . .	= He's got . . .
∨ She has got . . .	= She's got . . .
We have got . . .	= We've got . . .
You have got . . .	= You've got . . .
They have got . . .	= They've got . . .

Have you got your bag?
> Yes, I have. / No, I haven't.

Has Mr X got a white boat?
> Yes, he has. / No, he hasn't.

Check Look again at pages 40
and 56. Play the games.

✻ There is . . . There are . . .

There's one rabbit in my uncle's hat.
Now there are five rabbits in his hat.

Is there a dog in his hat?
> Yes, there is. / No, there isn't.

Check Look again at page 45.
Play the game.
Look again at page 47. Sing the song.

Are you a good detective?   *(Revision)*

⌣ 46 Can you remember?   Listen and point to the right picture.

Syllabus

Unit		Language items	Functions and topics
1	page 1	*Hello.* *Goodbye.* *What's your name?* *I'm . . .* *My name's Woody.* *Who's this?* *This is . . .* Possessives: *my / your.* The alphabet.	Greeting and saying farewell. Asking someone's name. Introducing yourself. Introducing others. Talking about possession.
2	page 5	*Listen, please.* *What's this?* Article: *a* + noun. *Good morning.* *How are you?* *I'm fine, thank you.*	Commands. Identifying things. Further greetings and responses.
3	page 9	Numbers 1–10. *How old are you?* *I'm ten.* *We're twins.* *This is 94312.* Article: *an* + a e i o u.	Counting. Talking about age. Telephone numbers.
4	page 13	*It's a kite.*	Naming common toys and household objects.
5	page 17	*He's seven.* *She's eight.* Possessives: *his / her.* Revision.	Talking about possession.
6	page 21	*Is it an aeroplane?* *Yes, it is. / No, it isn't.* Article: *the* + noun. Adjectives: *the big / small box.*	Asking for information. Specifying particular objects.
7	page 25	*I've got a big nose.* *This is my mother.* *She's got big eyes.* *We've got a letter.*	Describing people: faces and hair. Members of the family.

Syllabus continued

Unit		Language items	Functions and topics
8	page 29	*Have you got your bag?* *Yes, I have./No, I haven't.* *Has she got her umbrella?* *Yes, she has./No, she hasn't.* Adjectives: *tall, short,* etc.	Asking for information. Describing people.
9	page 33	*Can you see an elephant?* *Yes, I can./No, I can't.* *Whose cage is this?* Possessive___'s: *the lion's cage.* *Turn right, turn left.*	Talking about ability. Talking about possession. Zoo animals. Giving directions.
10	page 37	*Show me the green kite.* *What colour is her skirt?* *It's red.* Revision.	Colours. Clothes.
11	page 41	*He's got brown legs.* *He's from England.*	Parts of the body. Saying where people or things come from.
12	page 45	Plural nouns: *–s/–es.* *There's . . ./There are . . .* *Is there . . . ?* *Yes, there is./No, there isn't.* Prepositions: *in, on.*	Describing situations. Asking for information. Specifying location.
13	page 49	*How many monsters are there?* *How many . . . can you see?* Preposition: *at + the bank,* etc.	Asking about number. Shops and places in town.
14	page 53	*What time is it?* *It's twelve o'clock.* *At eleven o'clock . . .* *. . . in the morning/evening.*	Asking and telling the time. Specifying the time of day.
15	page 57	*Square, circle, triangle.* Revision.	Talking about shape.